THE PEAK DISTRICT
A WINTER'S TALE

ROBERT FALCONER

HALSGROVE

First published in Great Britain in 2009

British Library Cataloguing-in-Publication Data
A CIP record for this title is available from the British Library

ISBN 978 1 84114 908 0

HALSGROVE
Halsgrove House,
Ryelands Industrial Estate,
Bagley Road, Wellington, Somerset TA21 9PZ
Tel: 01823 653777   Fax: 01823 216796
email: sales@halsgrove.com

Part of the Halsgrove group of companies
Information on all Halsgrove titles is available at: www.halsgrove.com

Printed and bound in India on behalf of JFDi Print Services Ltd

INTRODUCTION

The air bites at your fingers and toes, the ground is hard under your feet and coated in a heavy layer of hoar frost. From a high viewpoint in the Peak District you are able to look down at the misty filled valley as the sun just manages to climb into the cold blue sky. This is just one scene that can be witnessed in the heart of winter.

The Peak District National Park is an area in Northern England of outstanding natural beauty. The High Peak in particular is a very dramatic, wild, unforgiving place at any time of the year. But it is in winter when these qualities can be seen to full effect, and for me the best time to capture these elements with my camera.

I have travelled to many interesting places in the world, but being born and living just a few miles from the northeast corner of the park has made me focus much of my time trying to express all the moods of the Peak.

Winter is often many people's least favourite season. Climate change is something very much in the headlines these days. Fears of global warming could change our seasons forever. But no season is ever the same and they can often merge into each other, sometimes starting early or ending later than expected. It is not uncommon for snow to fall while the golden leaves of autumn are still on the trees or for spring flowers to be given a shock by a late frost or fall of snow. But officially winter starts just a few days before Christmas, when many people are hoping for snow and dreaming of a white Christmas. In the last two decades since I started photographing the Peak District we have managed a few white Christmases, especially in the High Peak. A covering of snow amongst the Christmas lights can create a very beautiful scene. Winter then marches on through January and February, finishing in the middle of March. But on occasions snow can be seen on the high peaks, briefly, as late as April.

Winter can be a very gloomy season, cold and wet, but it can also be one of my favourite times of year. It is a time when you can create some of the most stunning landscape images. Dramatic looking skies can have a very powerful impact in a picture. When the sun does shine it remains low in the sky all day, helping to bring out the textures and shapes in the landscape. The landscape itself can look dead and bleak as it waits in hibernation for the warmer weather to arrive. There may seem to be no colour in the landscape but if you look carefully you can find many shades of browns and greens. To me the trees look very dramatic at this time of year, as their branches are bare, showing off their shapes in great silhouette, like a skeleton. Trees can look even more like a skeleton just after a snowfall as the flakes cling onto the branches until the winter sun thaws the trees.

The one element that we associate most with winter is snow. A covering of snow can completely change the look of a landscape and change an ordinary scene into something quite magical. These days snow rarely falls in the low-lying areas and when it does it can go as quickly as it arrives. But few winters go by without the High Peak being transformed into a winter wonderland.

It is not normally cold enough to freeze our lakes and rivers but it can still be possible to find interesting ice formations, nature's own way of creating sculpture in the landscape. These can be found during periods of cold temperatures on the edges of small streams running off the moors and hills. There is no shortage of cloudy days in winter and these provide the best light to photograph the ice, the soft light reflecting through the ice creating great effects for photography. When I am around water I normally wear my wellingtons so I can get up close to the ice, often with my tripod right in the middle of the stream. There are many streams that run off Kinder Scout and I have seen some icicles clinging to the slopes up to two metres long.

We may not be in the Arctic but you have to take the wintry conditions seriously. Be prepared for harsh conditions and take extra care on the roads. I always have a spade in my car in case I become stuck and I always dress for the weather with many layers of clothes; you can't beat thermal underwear to keep you warm from the cold northerly winds!

There are some places in the Peak District which I love to visit time and time again, not just in winter but also throughout the seasons. No visit is ever the same; the light and weather conditions always bring up new opportunities and the more you see a place the more you see things that appeared invisible before. Three places I never get tired of photographing are Curbar Edge, Mam Tor and Stanage Edge.

A great deal of thought has gone into my selection of images for this book. It is not meant as a guide to the Peak in winter but a personal winter journey I have taken over the last twenty years. With global warming in people's minds these days there have been many predictions for the future of our environment. As the planet becomes warmer these scenes of snow and ice could become archive material.

I always get excited when snow is forecast and winter dominates my Peak District collection.

There were a few factors I considered when choosing the pictures to use from my collection in the book. Firstly I wanted to try and cover as large an area of the Peak District as possible, but even though I have been taking pictures of the Peak for many years, there are still areas I have not explored yet.

I also wanted to show as big a variety of moods as possible, which can be seen in the winter months. The weather in winter can be very changeable and extreme. It often appears that we get everything including the kitchen sink thrown at us in winter. I have tried to capture all of these conditions in my pictures – apart from a kitchen sink.

The pictures in the book show occasions from beautiful crystal clear days with cold blue skies to overcast dull days when waterfalls and ice formations still seem to glisten in what light is available. Also days when the landscape turns white, from a thick coating of frost or dusting of snow to a deep blanket of snow. Atmospheric days too with mist or fog. I have also tried to show the effect the wind can have, with the snow being blown across the hills and the sculptured drifts that are left behind. All these conditions show that there is a picture to be had at anytime during winter.

In the pictures I have tried to show a variety of different times of day. The light is always changing and you can get different effects in the mornings and afternoons. There are pictures taken from before sunrise to sunset and on into the night. My favourite time of day is dawn. I never get tired of looking east to see the first glimmer of the sun

appear above the horizon. It can also be the coldest time of day, before the sun warms the ground to melt the frost or evaporate the mist.

With the subjects too, I have tried to show variety. I did not want to just portray the bleakness of winter and the wild remote landscapes that can be found in the Peak, but I also wanted to show the villages and people in the Park, to show that the Peak District is not just a nature reserve but also a place in which people live, work and play.

From the farmer crossing the landscape in his tractor, people enjoying a winter walk and admiring the beautiful surroundings to people having lots of fun sledging on the snowy slopes. You can view my pictures from the warmth of your own home.

The gateway to the UK's first National Park, an area of stunning beauty and
contrasts, made even more dramatic in winter.

As day turns to night, Castleton comes alive with its beautiful Christmas lights along the High Street. A covering of snow adds to the festive scene.

Castleton is a magical place at Christmas and has one of the best displays of
Christmas lights in the Peak District.

As the sky darkens and with a covering of snow in the churchyard, the lights on the trees make a very festive scene at Baslow church.

A snowman stands proud, high above the Hope Valley and he even managed to smile for the camera.

(Right) The setting sun turns the sky into a blaze of colour over Parsley Hay.

Looking across Gradbach to the patchwork of fields and farms with the distinctive peak of Shutlingsloe looming above.

(Right) Looking down the escarpment of The Roaches towards Hen Cloud and beyond across the Staffordshire countryside. The Roaches makes a dramatic natural barrier on the western edge of the Peak District.

These gritstone rocks on the northern edge of The Roaches have been shaped over thousands of years by nature. Little pockets of snow shelter at their base.

A road snakes its way on the banks of the Upper Dove between Crowdecote and Longnor, catching the afternoon light.

Looking north up the Upper Dove Valley from Crowdecote towards the unmistakeable shape of Chrome Hill.

Parkhouse Hill catches the sun on a winter afternoon.

The medieval field sytems stand out in the snow above Chelmorton.

All appears quiet in the centre of Monyash on a cold winter morning.

Early morning light glistens on the Bulls Head pub, which is at the heart of Monyash.

(Right) Monyash church is reflected in the village pond, as snow lies on the ground.

An open gateway on Taddington Moor leads your eye into the snow-covered field.

Clouds streak across the deep blue sky adding great contrast to the snow-covered
landscape high up on the White Peak plateau.

Two trees stand against a menacing sky on a bleak Bradwell Moor.

A tractor heads home past the patchwork of dry-stone walls near Flagg.

Near the village of Sheldon, Magpie Mine stands as a monument to a once thriving lead mine industry and it is now the best preserved mine in the Peak District.

First light hits the fields looking towards Gib Hill, which is a Neolithic burial mound with a Bronze Age mound on top.

The first rays of sun light up Arbor Low, one of the most important prehistoric sites in the Peak District.

A close up of one of the fallen prehistoric stones which make up the henge of Arbor Low.

The red sphere of the sun heads towards the distinctive horizon of Mininglow Hill, which is the site of an ancient burial ground and can been seen for miles across the Peak District.

(Right) As the sun struggles to burn through the early morning fog, the Bronze Age stones on Harthill Moor make a mysterious silhouette. There are four stones now remaining from an original nine.

The unusual-shaped rocks of Robin Hood's Stride, on the edge of Harthill Moor,
are outlined against a spectacular sunrise.

Legend has it that Robin Hood leapt from stone to stone to escape the Sheriff
of Nottingham.

The impressive church in Youlgrave stands out against the winter landscape.

Bakewell church stands out on the skyline as the late afternoon light is reflected in the River Wye.

On a cold misty morning a child is walked to school across
a field at the edge of Bakewell.

The River Wye meanders through the deep valley between Monsal Dale and Ashford-in-the-Water on a very atmospheric morning.

Using a slow shutter speed helps to portray the moving water over the weir in Monsal Dale.

Standing high above the fog on Great Longstone Edge, a group of trees manage to pierce through into the early morning sunlight.

The beautiful old cottages of Litton catch the cold light on a January morning.

With the water in the village pond freezing over, the old chapel at Foolow is reflected in the pond.

The deep dale of Cressbrook Dale is covered in snow. The outcrop of rock in the top left is called Peters Stone.

The Peak is full of winding narrow roads. Here the road leads your eye up to the
village of Foolow.

The criss-cross of dry-stone walls make a patchwork pattern as far as the eye can see near Wardlow.

(Right) A view looking down from Eyam Edge at the misty and frosty landscape near Foolow.

The outline of Eyam church stands out against the winter sky as snow covers the ground.

The impressive Chatsworth House bathed in golden light as the shadows start to lengthen across the valley.

The slopes of Chatsworth Park near the village of Edensor are perfect for sledging,
and the first sign of snow attracts people from miles around for a bit of winter fun.

Chatsworth Park, alongside the River Derwent, is a lovely place for a walk at any
time of the year.

The village of Baslow nestles on the northern edge of the Chatsworth estate and is
seen here under a blanket of snow.

You would not normally look twice at the side of the road into Baslow, but the scene has been transformed by the snow.

The late afternoon light shines on the snow-covered hills around the edge of Baslow.

Standing high above Baslow on Baslow Edge is Wellington's Monument, erected
in 1866, which commemorates the Duke of Wellington who defeated Napoleon at
the Battle of Waterloo.

Across the valley on Birchen Edge is Nelson's Monument, which commemorates
Lord Nelson and his famous victory at the Battle of Trafalgar.

Just a stone's throw from Nelson's Monument are three gritstone rocks, with the names of Nelson's three most famous ships carved into the stone, *Victory, Defiant* and *Royal Soverin.*

Nelson's Monument is perched on the edge of Birchen Edge in a winter wonderland.

Looking west from Birchen Edge towards Baslow and beyond.

At the base of Birchen Edge, looking up through the snow-covered branches towards the deep blue sky.

The young silver birch trees look just like skeletons with their branches covered in snow.

Right on the eastern border of the Peak District the sun heads for the horizon over
Beeley Moor, casting a warm glow across the snowy landscape.

The low late-afternoon sun shines through the ice-coated landscape making the trees and the fence look like they are glowing.

This rickety old gate is transformed into an attractive sculpture as it is encased in ice catching the golden light.

(*Right*) Ice-covered branches glisten from the setting sun on Eastmoor making it look like the tree is full of fairy lights.

In the twilight afterglow the snow turns an attractive shade of blue at an open gateway on Eastmoor.

A very cold winter's day on the wild landscape of Eastmoor.

Young silver birch trees reach for the sky on the bleak eastern moorland near Baslow, as the setting sun turns the sky red.

The moorland fog starts to evaporate to reveal a frosty landscape on Leash Fen.

The rocks high up on Curbar Edge stand out against the misty landscape in the valley below.

Just below Curbar Edge a millstone is coated in frost crystals overlooking the misty landscape below.

The fog laps around the trees and houses on the edge of the village of Curbar.

(Left) A half-buried millstone on top of Curbar Edge catches the low morning light.

The twisting road descending from Curbar Edge
into the village of Curbar is paved with golden
light.

(*Left*) The stubborn fog refuses to clear in the
valley below Curbar Edge, catching the late,
golden afternoon light.

Curbar Edge and neighbouring Baslow Edge stand under a covering of snow.

At dawn on a very atmospheric day as the mist skirts Curbar Edge and the frost-coated stones.

The landscape above Froggatt Edge is made into an attractive setting after an over-night snowfall.

The path on top of Froggatt Edge moves away from the rocks at one point and
through an area of silver birch trees, which here have been transformed by a
blanket of snow.

High on Big Moor a lone silver birch has been shaped by the elements as it struggles to grow in this exposed landscape.

Looking across the frozen lake towards Longshaw Lodge in Longshaw Country Park owned by the National Trust.

The branches of an isolated tree in the Longshaw Country Park stand out against
the blue sky.

The snow-covered trees in the Longshaw Country Park make a natural tunnel.

When the temperature drops, ice is formed on the edge of the streams running off the High Peak moors creating interesting sculptures such as this one in Padley Gorge.

Icicles look like threatening teeth in Padley Gorge. To get close enough for the picture I had to stand in the middle of the stream in my wellingtons.

At Surprise View just east of Hathersage you get a great view looking down the
Hope Valley towards Castleton.

The dawn light picks out the features on the moorland as Higger Tor
looms on the horizon.

Centuries of wind and rain have chiselled out interesting shapes in the gritstone boulders, which were abandoned by the Ice Age. Here the first light of day bathes the landscape from Over Owler Tor to Winyards Nick and beyond to Stanage Edge.

Over Owler Tor is a group of exposed gritstone rocks which have commanding views across the High Peak moors and the Hope Valley.

The sun penetrates through the mist on the Whim Plantation situated below Millstone Edge at the east end of the Hope Valley.

The Hope Valley mist skirts round Mitchell Field Farm above Hathersage on a
cold frosty day.

Hand-crafted dry-stone walls have helped shape the landscape of the Peak District.
Here above Mitchell Field Farm the wall makes a dramatic arc before heading
down towards the farm.

Part of the dry-stone wall has been breached and is here covered by snow. Maintaining the walls is a very time consuming job.

The frost keeps a foothold on the rocks around Higger Tor as the distant Hope
Valley is filled with mist.

The last rays of sun turn the white snow pink on Higger Tor.

Looking down from Higger Tor, Carl Wark – which is also the site of a Roman fort – looks very mysterious in the mist.

In the High Peak the arctic conditions have a firm hold on a fence at the side of a road.

The setting sun casts a warm glow across a drift, picking out the textures
in the snow.

Overstones Farm is perched high above the Hope Valley at the eastern end of Stanage Edge, next to a patchwork of fields belonging to the farm.

A ray of sunlight shines down on Overstones Farm just minutes after a raging
blizzard had passed by.

The criss-cross of dry-stone walls next to Overstones Farm make a green abstract in the afternoon winter light.

A covering of snow completely changes the look of the fields into a monochromatic pattern.

A group of abandoned millstones make an interesting foreground at the
foot of Stanage Edge.

With the millstone submerged in snow, the sky turns black with the threat of more snow to come, looking east from Stanage Edge.

(Left) The setting sun gives the sky a warm tint over Stanage Edge.

Stanage Edge is a very popular place to visit for rock climbing, walking, or just to admire the view across the Peak District.

A balancing gritstone boulder makes a natural window on top of Stanage
Edge. It is sometimes hard to image how nature has created this wild and
beautiful landscape.

Stanage Edge is a high ridge of gritstone across the High Peak over 3 miles long where stunning views across the Hope Valley, Kinder, Bleaklow and the upper Derwent Valley can be found.

In the High Peak you can often hear the unmistakable sound of the red grouse. It sounds like it is heckling and laughing at you for being out in such a wild landscape.

Amongst the golden bracken a tree manages to take a foothold on the slopes below
Stanage Edge as a winter storm develops in the west.

Fog above Bamford in the Hope Valley gives a very eerie feel to a group of trees.

Mam Tor stands majestic above the mist at the western edge of the Hope Valley
seen here from Stanage Edge.

A bright red life-buoy is in stark contrast to the white landscape on the edge of Ladybower Reservoir.

In the 1930s, in the Upper Derwent Valley, work started on 3 large dams and 3 reservoirs to provide drinking water to nearby towns and cities. This impressive viaduct was also built to cross Ladybower Reservoir to carry the main Sheffield to Manchester road, seen here in silhouette at dawn.

The snowy hills around Ladybower Reservoir are perfectly reflected in the water.

Most of the snow has melted on the hills around the very still water of
Ladybower Reservoir.

In cold temperatures, around the edge of Ladybower Reservoir, interesting ice patterns have formed.

As the snow melts or after heavy rain you can feel the full force of the water as it pours over the top of Derwent Dam. As well as making an impressive sight it also makes a deafening sound.

On the edge of an inlet of Howden Reservoir the combination of pine trees and snow create an almost Canadian feel to the scene.

Derwent Edge provides a commanding vantage point overlooking Ladybower
Reservoir and across to Kinder Scout.

Fair Brook runs down into the Snake Pass valley. The brown colour of the water comes from the peat bogs on top of Kinder Scout.

The sun does not reach the ice and snow at the bottom of Cave Dale as the
Norman Peveril Castle is perched above the dale.

Winnats Pass is a spectacular natural feature in the Peak District, which once lay at the bottom of an ancient ocean. It is made even more magical by the swirling mist.

A group of trees below Mam Tor catch the pre-dawn light after a
fresh overnight snowfall.

A howling gale blows the snow over the hills towards a farm situated at the top of
Winnats Pass.

Looking east across the Hope Valley from the edge of Mam Tor, just after daybreak.

Mam Tor dominates the western end of the Hope Valley. Its constantly eroding
eastern face gives it the nickname 'Shivering Mountain'.

The cement works near Castleton can be seen for miles around and even
with the Hope Valley filled with fog it still managed to pierce through in
the pre dawn glow.

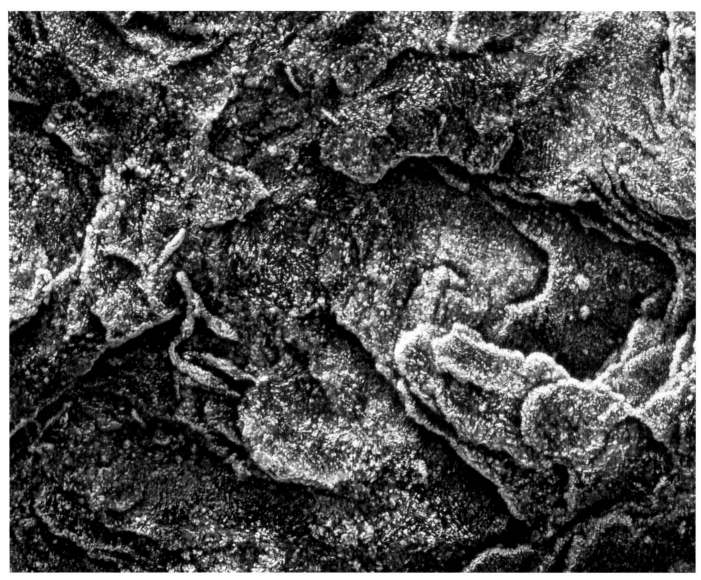

Sometimes a good picture will appear at your feet. A covering of hoar frost coupled with the early morning sunlight makes an attractive pattern on the flagstones that make up the main path on top of Mam Tor. These stones were brought in by helicopter by the National Trust to combat erosion.

The landscape is bathed in warm light just minutes after sunrise, looking along
the path from Mam Tor to Back Tor and Lose Hill.

Looking west from Mam Tor, the road to Chapel-en-le-Frith can be seen heading through the white landscape.

The freshly fallen snow along Rushup Edge makes an interesting pattern.

You can see the effects of the wind on this tree as it struggles to grow in its
exposed position on Rushup Edge.

The full moon starts to set over Edale and Kinder Scout as the sky
lightens before dawn.

On a bright winter's day, looking towards Jacobs Ladder, which is the first climb
north on the Pennine Way.

A lone tree is silhouetted against the dawn sky at the foot of Jacobs Ladder
looking towards Mam Tor.

Looking across Edale from The Nab towards Lose Hill and Win Hill further in
the distance.

Each individual blade of grass is coated in ice at the side of Grinds Brook just outside the village of Edale.

In the cold temperatures at the side of Grinds Brook, which runs off Kinder Scout, stunning formations of ice can be found, with some of them up to two metres long.

Heavy snow falls around the village of Edale.

After a steep climb from Edale the view from Ringing Roger is well worth it.

The side of Kinder Scout climbs steeply up from Edale, bathed in afternoon sunshine.

A walker pauses to admire the view across Edale and beyond, at Nether Tor on Kinder Scout.

Kinder Scout is the highest point in the Peak District and after a snowfall the wind gets a chance to create interesting shapes in the snow at the top of Jacobs Ladder.

The Wool Packs is a collection of gritstone boulders of all shapes and sizes making an alien-looking landscape. Some of them have names such as this one which is called The Snail. All can be found on the southern edge of Kinder Scout plateau.

Windswept snowdrifts form the foreground on a wild winter's day on Kinder Scout.

One of the first lambs of the coming spring wonders what all this white stuff is on
the ground with the last snow of winter covering the upper Derwent Valley.